D1562142

CHIEF JOSEPH

Chief Joseph (1840-1904), war leader of the Nez Perce Indians in the 1870s, was a military genius. In 1877, when his tribe was driven from its homeland by forces of white settlers, Chief Joseph led men, women and children more than 1500 miles through the Montana wilderness for escape to Canada. Captured near the border by the U.S. Army, exiled with his people to the bitter country of Indian Territory, Chief Joseph worked tirelessly for peace. He won a return to the Northwest for his Nez Perce in 1885. They were confined on the Colville Reservation in Northeast Washington. Chief Joseph forgave his enemies and was a peacemaker to the day of his death. He is buried at Nespelem.

Erected by the Washington State Highway Commission

CHIEF JOSEPH'S OWN STORY

YOUNG CHIEF JOSEPH
In-mut-too-yah-lat-lat (Rolling Thunder)
1840(?) - 9-22-1904

CHIEF JOSEPH'S

OWN STORY

Ye Galleon Press
Fairfield, Washington
2004

Library of Congress Cataloging in Publication Data

Joseph, Nez Perce Chief, 1840-1904.
    Cheif Joseph's own story.

    Reprint. Originally published: St. Paul, 1925.
        Includes bibliographical references
        1. Nez Perce Indians—Wars, 1877—Personal narratives. 2. Joseph,
Nez Perce Chief, 1840-1904. I. Title.
E83.877.J79   1984   973.8'3   81-19644
ISBN 0-87770-261-6   AACR2

Reprinted 2004

CHIEF JOSEPH

Photo credit. Washington State University, Pullman, WA.
L.V. McWhorter Collection.

Chief Joseph

Chief Joseph's Last Stand

Young Joseph, his people, and his marvelous retreat of nearly two thousand miles.

FOREWORD

By DONALD MACRAE

About fifteen miles to the south of the Great Northern Railway tracks at Chinook, Montana, a historic battlefield lies almost forgotten among the ravines and gullies that line the high bluffs of Snake Creek near its junction with the Milk River in the Bear Paw Mountains. Its trenches and earth works have gradually fallen into decay and the wild flowers and tall prairie grass have nearly obliterated the graves of its heroic dead.

Few people today, save possibly those living close by or those interested in Northwest history, can tell you the name of this place or of those who so gallantly fought here; yet less than fifty years ago on this very spot the white man and the red were fighting one of their last great battles.

Chief Joseph and his band of Nez Percé warriors had successfully defeated General Howard's men on the Lolo trail, fought a drawn battle with General Gibbon at Big Hole and were rapidly retreating by a circuitous trail to join Sitting Bull in Canada, but the telegraph of the white man was working against him. Unknown to this Indian Chieftain, Colonel (later General) Miles was rapidly marching to the Northwest to intercept him before he could reach the border. Had Chief Joseph known of this he could have easily escaped with all his people as he crossed the Missouri a full day ahead of Miles, but the Three Daughters of the Night decreed otherwise and the opposing forces met at this spot on the 30th of September, 1877.

Three days later General Howard arrived upon the scene and, on the 4th of October, Joseph surrendered with eighty-seven warriors, of whom forty were wounded, one hundred and eighty-four squaws and one hundred and forty-seven children. This was the pathetic message of surrender he sent to General Howard:

Tell General Howard that I know his heart. What he told me before—I have it in my heart. I am tired of fighting. Our chiefs are killed. Looking Glass is dead. *Too-hul-hul-sote* is dead. The old men are all dead. It is the young men now, who say "yes" or "no" (that is, vote in council). He who led the young men (Joseph's brother Ollicut) is dead. It is cold, and we have no blankets. The little children are freezing to death. My people—some of them—have run away to the hills, and have no blankets, no food. No one knows where they are—perhaps freezing to death. I want to have time to look for my children, and to see how many of them I can find; maybe I shall find them among the dead. Hear me, my chiefs, my heart is sick and sad. From where the sun now stands, I will fight no more with the white man. [1]

This remarkable Indian had accomplished a feat that will be long remembered as a military exploit of the first magnitude. His small force, which at no time numbered more than three hundred warriors, had retreated for nearly two thousand miles through an enemy country, carrying with them their squaws and children. They had met United States troops eleven different times and had fought five pitched battles with them, of which they had won three, drew one and lost one, a feat that is more remarkable when you learn that the total force opposing them was nearly two thousand men. But greatest of all is the fact that this campaign was conducted without the destruction of property and the murdering of settlers that usually was a part of Indian warfare.

[1]*American Fights and Fighters, The Nez Perce War, by Cyrus Townsend Brady.*

Chief Joseph

Young Joseph—he bore this name for a long time as his father was also called Joseph—was the last of the great warrior chieftains. He was a wonderful specimen of the Indian, standing six feet tall, straight as an arrow and wonderfully handsome, his features being as clear-cut as chiseled marble. The New York Sun of September 24, 1904—in commenting on his death—says he was a great orator and though he never spoke a word of English some of his sayings, translated, have become famous. He is reported to have said—"Look twice at a two-faced man;" "Cursed be the hand that scalps the reputation of the dead;" "The eye tells what the tongue would hide;" "Big name often stands on small legs;" "Finest fur may cover toughest meat."[2]

[2] In early years when the young Joseph appeared before the government commission to plead for his people and his lands, the commissioners were amazed at his wonderful oratorical powers. This seemed to be a natural gift among the Indians. At the Portage des Sioux (the point of land lying between the confluence of the Missouri with the Mississippi) where, in 1815, a treaty was signed which pacified the western Indians, Standing Elk, the great chief of the Maha nation, delivered his historic address over the grave of the Teton chief, Black Buffalo. "Do not grieve," said the red orator, upon that occasion, "misfortune will happen to the wisest and best men. Death will come, and always comes out of season; it is the command of the Great Spirit, and all nations and people must obey. What is past, and cannot be prevented, should not be grieved for. Be not discouraged or displeased then, that in visiting your father here you have lost your chief. A misfortune of this kind may never again befall you; but this would have attended you perhaps in your own village. Five times have I visited this land, and never returned with sorrow or pain. Misfortunes do not flourish particularly in our path, they grow everywhere. (Addressing himself to Governor Edwards and Colonel Miller): What a misfortune for me that I could not have died this day, instead of the chief that lies before us. The trifling loss my nation would have sustained in my death would have been doubly paid for by the honors of my burial—they would have wiped off everything like regret. Instead of being covered with a cloud of sorrow, my warriors would have let the sunshine of joy in their hearts. To me it would have been a most glorious occurrence. Hereafter, when I die at home, instead of a noble grave and a grand procession, the rolling music and the thundering cannon, with a flag waving at my head, I shall be wrapped in a robe (an old robe, perhaps) and hoisted on a slender scaffold to the whistling winds, soon to be blown down to the earth; my flesh to be devoured by wolves, and my bones rattled on the plain by the wild beasts. (Addressing himself to Col. Miller): Chief of the soldiers, your labors have not been in vain; your attentions shall not be forgotten, my nation shall know the respect that is paid over the dead. When I return I will echo the sound of your guns."

Of his early life not much is known save that he was born in eastern Oregon about 1840. He was the eldest of Old Joseph's two sons and the hereditary chief of the Lower Nez Percé Indians. His early childhood was most likely spent learning the usual war and hunting arts common to his people though he did spend some time at Rev. Spaulding's school—Rev. Spaulding was a missionary who spent many years among the Nez Percé Indians.

From his father he learned to be careful when dealing with the whites and to never sell or sign away the lands of his people. This he never did and it was cause of his taking charge of the "non-treaty" Indians and consummating his marvelous retreat through the fastness of the Rockies and over the Montana plains nearly to the Canadian border; although he took no part in the massacres that were the immediate cause of the outbreak.

This retreat was a masterpiece of military strategy, his men often holding superior forces at bay while a small detachment of them slipped around one side and cut off the enemies' supplies. His warriors—although the Nez Percés had been at peace for years—were perfectly trained in all the arts of war; in fact, at one time he formed forty of his men in columns of four and in the dusk of early night pulled a surprise attack on Howard's troops—the sentry thinking, by their orderly formation, that they were part of General Howard's cavalry. General O. O. Howard in his book about the Nez Percé and Joseph's retreat says of this particular instance that, "At the Camas Meadows, not far from Henry Lake, Joseph's night march, his surprise of my camp and capture of over a hundred animals, and, after a slight battle, making a successful escape, showed an ability to plan and execute equal to that of many a partisan leader whose deeds have entered into classic story."

Even in his last battle he held out for four days against a force that out-numbered his two to one and his quiet dignity and forbearance at the time of his surrender won him the respect and friendship of General Miles.

"Thus," says General Sherman, speaking of Joseph's surrender to General Miles, "has terminated one of the most extraordinary Indian wars of which there is any record. The Indians throughout displayed a courage and skill that elicited universal praise; they abstained from scalping, let captive women go free, did not commit indiscriminate murder of peaceful families, which is usual, and fought with almost scientific skill, using advance and rear guards, skirmish lines and field fortifications."[3]

After his surrender, he and his people were sent to Fort Leavenworth and later to Baxter Springs, Kansas. In these places many of the Indians died but it wasn't until 1885 that the sorry remnant of this audacious band was sent to spend the remainder of their lives on the Colville reservation, in northern Washington; a country similar to their beloved Valley of the Winding Waters and a place where they could live in peace in a climate that they were accustomed to.

For twelve years Chief Joseph lived quietly on this reservation but in 1897 becoming alarmed by the encroachments of the whites in their reservation he again took up the defense of his people, this time by going to Washington and pleading with the President. Again it was General Miles—the only white man that he believed and trusted—who promised him that his people would be unmolested in the lands they now occupied.

Returning to the reservation he again settled down to enjoy the peace and quiet of old age, making only one more trip, this time a friendly visit to the President and his old friend General Miles—for a part of the time during this trip he took part in Cummin's Indian Congress and Life on the Plains during that show's exhibition at the famous Madison Square Garden—and a year after this trip he dropped dead in front of his tepee on Sept. 22, 1904.

In speaking of his death, C. T. Brady, in his book about the Nez Percé War, says: "The other day a gray-headed old chief, nodding by the fire, dreaming perhaps of days of daring and deeds of valor, by which, savage though he was, he had written his name on the pages of history, slipped quietly to the ground and fell into his eternal sleep. Peaceful ending for the Indian Xenophon, the Red Napoleon of the West."[4]

3*Massacres of the Mountains, page 660, by J. P Dunn, Jr. Harper & Bros., 1886.*
4*Page 40, Northwestern Fights and Fighters, Cyrus Townsend Brady. Doubleday, Page & Co.*

Chief Joseph's Own Story

*With an Introduction by the Rt. Rev. W. H. Hare, D. D.,
Bishop of South Dakota**

I wish that I had words at command in which to express adequately the interest with which I have read the extraordinary narrative which follows, and which I have the privilege of introducing to the readers of this Review. I feel, however, that this

---

This story first appeared in The North American Review for April, 1879, and later in the book, Northwestern Fights and Fighters, written by Cyrus Townsend Brady. It is through the gracious permission of Messrs. Harper and Bros., the present publishers of The North American Review, and Doubleday, Page and Company, the publishers of Mr. Brady's book, that this story has been reproduced here.

apologia is so boldly marked by the charming naivete and tender pathos which characterizes the red man, that it needs no introduction, much less any authentication; while in its smothered fire, in its deep sense of eternal righteousness and of present evil, and in its hopeful longings for the coming of a better time, this Indian chief's appeal reminds us of one of the old Hebrew prophets of the days of the Captivity.

I have no special knowledge of the history of the Nez Percés, the Indians whose tale of sorrow Chief Joseph so pathetically tells —my Indian missions lying in a part at the West quite distant from their homes—and am not competent to judge their case upon its merits. The chief's narrative is, of course, ex parte, and many of his statements would no doubt be ardently disputed. General Howard, for instance, can hardly receive justice at his hands, so well known is he for his friendship to the Indian and for his distinguished success in pacifying some of the most desperate.

It should be remembered, too, in justice to the army, that it is rarely called upon to interfere in Indian affairs until the relations between the Indians and the whites have reached a desperate condition, and when the situation of affairs has become so involved and feeling on both sides runs so high that perhaps only more than human forbearance would attempt to solve the difficulty by disentangling the knot and not by cutting it.

Nevertheless, the chief's narrative is marked by so much candor, and he is so careful to qualify his statements, when qualification seems necessary, that every reader will give him credit for speaking his honest, even should they be thought by some to be mistaken, convictions. The chief, in his treatment of his defense, reminds one of those lawyers of whom we have heard that their splendid success was gained, not by disputation, but simply by their lucid and straightforward statement of their case. That he is something of a strategist as well as an advocate appears from this description of an event which occurred shortly after the breaking out of hostilities: "We crossed over Salmon River, hoping General Howard would follow. We were not disappointed. He did follow us, and we got between him and his supplies, and cut him off for three days." Occasionally the reader comes upon touches of those sentiments and feelings which at once establish a sense of kinship between all who possess them. Witness his description of his desperate attempt to rejoin his wife and children when a sudden dash of General Miles' soldiers had cut the Indian camp in two. . . . "I thought of my wife and children, who were now surrounded by soldiers, and I resolved to go to them. With a prayer in my mouth to the Great Spirit Chief who rules above, I dashed unarmed through the line of soldiers. . . My clothes were cut to pieces, my horse was wounded, but I was not hurt." And, again, when he speaks of his father's death: "I saw he was dying. I took his hand in mine. He said: 'My son, my body is returning to my mother earth, and my spirit is going very soon to see the Great Spirit Chief. . . . A few more years and the white men will be all around you. They have their eyes on this land. My son, never forget my dying words. This country holds your father's body—never sell the bones of your father and mother.' I pressed my father's hand, and told him I would protect his grave with my life. My father smiled, and passed away to the spirit land. I buried him in that beautiful valley of Winding Waters. I love that land more than all the rest of the world. A man who would not love his father's grave is worse than a wild animal."

His appeals to the natural rights of man are surprisingly fine, and, however some may despise them as the utterance of an Indian, they are just those which, in our Declaration of Independence, have been most admired. "We are all sprung from a woman," he says, "although we are unlike in many things. You are as you were made, and, as you are made, you can remain. We are just as we were made by the Great Spirit, and you cannot change us; then, why should children of one mother quarrel? Why should one try to cheat another? I do not believe that the Great Spirit Chief gave one kind of men the right to tell another kind of men what they must do."

But I will not detain the readers of the Review from the pleasure of perusing for themselves Chief Joseph's statement longer than is necessary to express the hope that those who have time for no more will at least read its closing paragraph, and to remark that the narrative brings clearly out these facts which ought to be regarded as well-recognized principles in dealing with the red man:

1. The folly of any mode of treatment of the Indian which

is not based upon a cordial and operative acknowledgment of his rights as our fellow-man.

2. The danger of riding roughshod over a people who are capable of high enthusiasm, who know and value their national rights, and are brave enough to defend them.

3. The liability to want of harmony between different departments and different officials of our complex Government, from which it results that, while many promises are made to the Indians, few of them are kept. It is a home-thrust when Chief Joseph says: "The white people have too many chiefs. They do not understand each other. . . . I cannot understand how the Government sends a man out to fight us, as it did General Miles, and then breaks his word. Such a Government has something wrong about it."

4. The unwisdom, in most cases, in dealing with Indians, of what may be termed military short-cuts, instead of patient discussion, explanations, persuasion, and reasonable concessions.

5. The absence in an Indian tribe of any truly representative body competent to make a treaty which shall be binding upon all the bands. The failure to recognize this fact has been the source of endless difficulties. Chief Joseph, in this case, did not consider a treaty binding which his band had not agreed to, no matter how many other bands had signed it; and so it has been in many other cases.

6. Indian chiefs, however able and influential, are really without power, and for this reason, as well as others, the Indians, when by the march of events they are brought into intimate relations with the whites, should at the earliest practicable moment be given the support and protection of our Government and of our law; not local law, however, which is apt to be the result of special legislation adopted solely in the interest of the stronger race.

WILLIAM H. HARE.

Chief Joseph's Story

*Told by him on his trip to Washington, D. C., in 1897.**

My friends, I have been asked to show you my heart. I am glad to have a chance to do so. I want the white people to understand my people. Some of you think an Indian is like a wild animal. This is a great mistake. I will tell you all about our people, and then you can judge whether an Indian is a man or not. I believe much trouble and blood would be saved if we opened our hearts more. I will tell you in my way how the Indian sees things. The white man has more words to tell you how they look to him, but it does not require many words to speak the truth. What I have to say will come from my heart, and I will speak with a straight tongue. Ah-cum-kin-i-ma-me-hut (the Great Spirit) is looking at me, and will hear me.

My name is In-mut-too-yah-lat-lat (Thunder-traveling-over-the-mountains). I am chief of the Wal-lam-wat-kin band of Chute-pa-lu, or Nez Percés (nose-pierced Indians). I was born in eastern Oregon, thirty-eight winters ago. My father was chief before me. When a young man he was called Joseph by Mr. Spaulding, a missionary. He died a few years ago. There was no stain on his hands of the blood of a white man. He left a good name on the earth. He advised me well for my people.

Our fathers gave us many laws, which they had learned from their fathers. These laws were good. They told us to treat all men as they treated us; that we should never be the first to break a bargain; that it was a disgrace to tell a lie; that we should speak only the truth; that it was a shame for one man to take from another his wife, or his property, without paying for it. We were taught to believe that the Great Spirit sees and hears everything, and that He never forgets; that hereafter He will give every man a spirit-home according to his deserts; if he has been a good man, he will have a good home; if he has been a bad man, he will have a bad home. This I believe, and all my people believe the same.

We did not know there were other people besides the Indians until about one hundred winters ago, when some men with white faces came to our country. They brought many things with them

*Chief Joseph's story is presented here not as a matter of historic record or as evidence in the controversy over the facts in connection with the treaty of 1855, but to give an impression of the character of the man. Space will not permit including General Howard's reply, which appears in Cyrus Townsend Brady's book, "Northwestern Fights and Fighters."

to trade for furs and skins. They brought tobacco, which was new to us. They brought guns with flint-stones on them, which frightened our women and children. Our people could not talk with these white-faced men, but they used signs which all people understood. These men were Frenchmen, and they called our people "Nez Percés," because they wore rings in their noses for ornaments. Although very few of our people wear them now, we are still called by the same name. These French trappers said a great many things to our fathers, which have been planted in our hearts. Some were good for us, but some were bad. Our people were divided in opinion about these men. Some thought they taught more bad than good. An Indian respects a brave man, but he despises a coward. He loves a straight tongue, but he hates a forked tongue. The French trappers told us some truths and some lies.

The first white men of your people who came to our country were named Lewis and Clarke. They also brought many things that our people had never seen. They talked straight, and our people gave them a great feast, as a proof that their hearts were friendly. These men were very kind. They made presents to our chiefs and our people made presents to them. We had a great many horses of which we gave them what they needed, and they gave us guns and tobacco in return. All the Nez Percés made friends with Lewis and Clarke, and agreed to let them pass through their country, and never to make war on white men. This promise the Nez Percés have never broken. No white man can accuse them of bad faith, and speak with a straight tongue. It has always been the pride of the Nez Percés that they were the friends of the white men. When my father was a young man there came to our country a white man (Rev. Mr. Spaulding) who talked spirit law. He won the affections of our people because he spoke good things to them. At first he did not say anything about white men wanting to settle on our lands. Nothing was said about that until about twenty winters ago when a number of white people came into our country and built houses and made farms. At first our people made no complaint. They thought there was room enough for all to live in peace, and they were learning many things from the white men that seemed to be good. But we soon found that the white men were growing rich very fast, and were greedy to possess everything the Indian had. My father was the first to see through the schemes of the white men, and he warned his tribe to be careful about trading with them. He had a suspicion of men who seemed so anxious to make money. I was a boy then, but I remember well my father's caution. He had sharper eyes than the rest of our people.

Next there came a white officer (Governor Stevens) who invited all the Nez Percés to a treaty council. After the council was opened he made known his heart. He said there were a great many white people in the country, and many more would come; that he wanted the land marked out so that the Indians and white men could be separated. If they were to live in peace it was necessary, he said, that the Indians should have a country set apart for them, and in that country they must stay. My father, who represented his band, refused to have anything to do with the council, because he wished to be a free man. He claimed that no man owned any part of the earth, and a man could not sell what was not his own.

Mr. Spaulding took hold of my father's arm and said: "Come and sign the treaty." My father pushed him away and said: "Why do you ask me to sign away my country? It is your business to talk to us about spirit matters, and not to talk to us about parting with our land." Governor Stevens urged my father to sign his treaty, but he refused. "I will not sign your paper," he said, "you go where you please, so do I; you are not a child, I am no child; I can think for myself. No man can think for me. I have no other home than this. I will not give it up to any man. My people would have no home. Take away your paper. I will not touch it with my hand."

My father left the council. Some of the chiefs of the other bands of the Nez Percés signed the treaty, and then Governor Stevens gave them presents of blankets. My father cautioned his people to take no presents, for "after awhile," he said, "they will claim that you accepted pay for your country." Since that time four bands of Nez Percés have received annuities from the United States. My father was invited to many councils, and they tried hard to make him sign the treaty, but he was firm as the rock, and would not sign away his home. His refusal caused a difference among the Nez Percés.

Eight years later (1863) was the next treaty council. A chief called Lawyer, because he was a great talker, took the lead in this council, and sold nearly all of the Nez Percé country. My father was not there. He said to me: "When you go into council with the white man, always remember your country. Do not give it away. The white man will cheat you out of your home. I have taken no pay from the United States. I have never sold our land." In this treaty Lawyer acted without authority from our band. He had no right to sell the Wallowa (winding water) country. That had always belonged to my father's own people, and the other bands had never disputed our right to it. No other Indians ever claimed Wallowa.

In order to have all people understand how much land we owned, my father planted poles around it and said:

"Inside is the home of my people—the white man may take the land outside. Inside this boundary all our people were born. It circles around the graves of our fathers, and we will never give up these graves to any man."

The United States claimed they had bought all the Nez Percés country outside the Lapwai Reservation from Lawyer and other chiefs, but we continued to live on this land in peace until eight years ago, when white men began to come inside the bounds my father had set. We warned them against this great wrong, but they would not leave our land, and some bad blood was raised. The white man represented that we were going upon the war-path. They reported many things that were false.

The United States Government again asked for a treaty council. My father had become blind and feeble. He could no longer speak for his people. It was then I took my father's place as chief. In this council I made my first speech to white men. I said to the agent who held the council:

"I did not want to come to this council, but I came hoping that we could save blood. The white man has no right to come here and take our country. We have never accepted presents from the Government. Neither Lawyer nor any other chief had authority to sell this land. It has always belonged to my people. It came unclouded to them from our fathers, and we will defend this land as long as a drop of Indian blood warms the hearts of our men."

The agent said he had orders, from the Great White Chief at Washington, for us to go upon the Lapwai Reservation, and that if we obeyed he would help us in many ways. "You must move to the agency," he said. I answered him: "I will not. I do not need your help; we have plenty, and we are contented and happy if the white man will let us alone. The reservation is too small for so many people with all their stock. You can keep your presents; we can go to your towns and pay for all we need; we have plenty of horses and cattle to sell, and we won't have any help from you; we are free now; we can go where we please. Our fathers were born here. Here they lived, here they died, here are their graves. We will never leave them." The agent went away, and we had peace for awhile.

Soon after this my father sent for me. I saw he was dying. I took his hand in mine. He said: "My son, my body is returning to my mother earth, and my spirit is going very soon to see the Great Spirit Chief. When I am gone, think of your country. You are the chief of these people. They look to you to guide them. Always remember that your father never sold his country. You must stop your ears whenever you are asked to sign a treaty selling your home. A few years more, and white men will be all around you. They have their eyes on this land. My son, never forget my dying words. This country holds your father's body. Never sell the bones of your father and your mother." I pressed my father's hand and told him that I would protect his grave with my life. My father smiled and passed away to the spirit-land.

I buried him in that beautiful valley of winding waters. I love that land more than all the rest of the world. A man who would not love his father's grave is worse than a wild animal.

For a short time we lived quietly. But this could not last. White men had found gold in the mountains around the land of the winding water. They stole a great many horses from us, and we could not get them back because we were Indians. The white men told lies for each other. They drove off a great many of our cattle. Some white men branded our young cattle so they could claim them. We had no friend who would plead our cause before the law councils. It seemed to me that some of the white men in Wallowa were doing these things on purpose to get up a war. They knew that we were not strong enough to fight them.

I labored hard to avoid trouble and bloodshed. We gave up some of our country to the white men, thinking that then we could have peace. We were mistaken. The white man would not let us alone. We could have avenged our wrongs many times, but we did not. Whenever the Government has asked us to help them against other Indians, we have never refused. When the white men were few and we were strong we could have killed them off, but the Nez Percés wished to live at peace.

If we have not done so, we have not been to blame. I believe that the old treaty has never been correctly reported. If we ever owned the land we own it still, for we never sold it. In the treaty councils the commissioners have claimed that our country had been sold to the Government. Suppose a white man should come to me and say, "Joseph, I like your horses, and I want to buy them." I say to him, "No, my horses suit me, I will not sell them." Then he goes to my neighbor, and says to him: "Joseph has some good horses. I want to buy them, but he refuses to sell." My neighbor answers, "Pay me the money, and I will sell you Joseph's horses." The white man returns to me and says, "Joseph, I have bought your horses, and you must let me have them." If we sold our lands to the Government, this is the way they were bought.

On account of the treaty made by the other bands of Nez Percés, the white men claimed my lands. We were troubled greatly by white men crowding over the line. Some of these were good men, and we lived on peaceful terms with them, but they were not all good.

Nearly every year the agent came over from Lapwai and ordered us on to the reservation. We always replied that we were satisfied to live in Wallowa. We were careful to refuse the presents or annuities which he offered.

Through all the years since the white man came to Wallowa we have been threatened and taunted by them and the treaty Nez Percés. They have given us no rest. We have had a few good friends among white men, and they have always advised my people to bear these taunts without fighting. Our young men were quick-tempered, and I have had great trouble in keeping them from doing rash things. I have carried a heavy load on my back ever since I was a boy. I learned then that we were but few, while the white men were many, and that we could not hold our own with them. We were like deer. They were like grizzly bears. We had a small country. Their country was large. We were contented to let things remain as the Great Spirit Chief made them. They were not; and would change the rivers and mountains if they did not suit them.

Year after year we have been threatened, but no war was made upon my people until General Howard came to our country two years ago and told us that he was the white war-chief of all that country. He said: "I have a great many soldiers at my back. I am going to bring them up here, and then I will talk to you again. I will not let white men laugh at me the next time I come. The country belongs to the Government, and I intend to make you go upon the reservation."

I remonstrated with him against bringing more soldiers to the Nez Percé country. He had one house full of troops all the time at Fort Lapwai.

The next spring the agent at Umatilla Agency sent an Indian runner to tell me to meet General Howard at Walla Walla. I could not go myself, but I sent my brother and five other head men to meet him, and they had a long talk.

General Howard said: "You have talked straight, and it is all right. You can stay at Wallowa." He insisted that my brother and his company should go with him to Fort Lapwai. When the party arrived there General Howard sent out runners and called all the Indians to a grand council. I was in that council. I said to General Howard, "We are ready to listen." He answered that he would not talk then, but would hold a council next day, when he would talk plainly. I said to General Howard: "I am ready to talk today. I have been in a great many councils, but I am no wiser. We are all sprung from a woman, although we are unlike in many things. We cannot be made over again. You are as you were made, and as you were made you can remain. We are just as we were made by the Great Spirit, and you cannot change us; then why should children of one mother and one father quarrel?— why should one try to cheat the other? I do not believe that the Great Spirit Chief gave one kind of men the right to tell another kind of men what they must do."

General Howard replied: "You deny my authority, do you? You want to dictate to me, do you?"

Then one of my chiefs—Too-hul-hul-sote—rose in the council and said to General Howard: "The Great Spirit Chief made the world as it is, and as He wanted it, and He made a part of it for us to live upon. I do not see where you get authority to say that we shall not live where He placed us."

General Howard lost his temper and said: "Shut up! I don't want to hear any more of such talk. The law says you shall go upon the reservation to live, and I want you to do so, but you persist in disobeying the law" (meaning the treaty). "If you do not move, I will take the matter into my own hand, and make you suffer for your disobedience."

Too-hul-hul-sote answered: "Who are you, that you ask us to talk, and then tell me I shan't talk? Are you the Great Spirit? Did you make the world? Did you make the sun? Did you make the rivers to run for us to drink? Did you make the grass to grow? Did you make all these things that you talk to us as though we were boys? If you did, then you have the right to talk as you do."

General Howard replied: "You are an impudent fellow, and I will put you in the guard-house," and then ordered a soldier to arrest him.

Too-hul-hul-sote made no resistance. He asked General Howard: "Is this your order? I don't care. I have expressed my heart to you. I have nothing to take back. I have spoken for my country. You can arrest me, but you cannot change me or make me take back what I have said."

The soldiers came forward and seized my friend and took him to the guard-house. My men whispered among themselves whether they would let this thing be done. I counseled them to submit. I knew if we resisted that all the white men present, including General Howard, would be killed in a moment, and we would be blamed. If I had said nothing, General Howard would never have given an unjust order against my men. I saw the danger and while they dragged Too-hul-hul-sote to prison, I arose and said: "I am going to talk now. I don't care whether you arrest me or not." I turned to my people and said: "The arrest of Too-hul-hul-sote was wrong, but we will not resent the insult. We were invited to this council to express our hearts, and we have done so."

Too-hul-hul-sote was prisoner for five days before he was released.

The council broke up that day. On the next morning General Howard came to my lodge, and invited me to go with him and White Bird and Looking Glass, to look for land for my people. As we rode along we came to some good land that was already occupied by Indians and white people. General Howard, pointing to this land, said: "If you will come on to the reservation, I will give you these lands and move these people off."

I replied: "No. It would be wrong to disturb these people. I have no right to take their home. I have never taken what did not belong to me. I will not now."

We rode all day upon the reservation, and found no good land unoccupied. I have been informed by men who do not lie that General Howard sent a letter that night telling the soldiers at Walla Walla to go to Wallowa Valley, and drive us out upon our return home.

In the council next day General Howard informed us in a haughty spirit that he would give my people thirty days to go back home, collect all their stock, and move on to the reservation, saying, "If you are not here in that time, I shall consider that you want to fight, and will send my soldiers to drive you on."

I said: "War can be avoided and it ought to be avoided. I want no war. My people have always been the friends of the white man. Why are you in such a hurry? I cannot get ready to move in thirty days. Our stock is scattered, and Snake River is very high. Let us wait until fall, then the river will be low. We want time to hunt our stock and gather our supplies for the winter."

General Howard replied, "If you let the time run over one day, the soldiers will be there to drive you on to the reservation, and all your cattle and horses outside of the reservation at that time will fall into the hands of the white men."

I knew I had never sold my country, and that I had no land in Lapwai; but I did not want bloodshed. T did not want my people killed. I did not want anybody killed. Some of my people had been murdered by white men, and the white murderers were never punished for it. I told General Howard about this, and again said I wanted no war. I wanted the people who live upon the lands I was to occupy at Lapwai to have time to gather their harvest.

I said in my heart that, rather than have war I would give up my country. I would rather give up my father's grave. I would give up everything rather than have the blood of white men upon the hands of my people.

General Howard refused to allow me more than thirty days to move my people and their stock. I am sure that he began to prepare for war at once.

When I returned to Wallowa I found my people very much excited upon discovering that the soldiers were already in the Wallowa Valley. We held a council, and decided to move immediately to avoid bloodshed.

Too-hul-hul-sote, who felt outraged by his imprisonment, talked for war, and made many of my young men willing to fight rather than be driven like dogs from the land where they were born. He declared that blood alone would wash out the disgrace General Howard had put upon him. It required a strong heart to stand up against such talk, but I urged my people to be quiet, and not to begin a war.

We gathered all the stock we could find, and made an attempt to move. We left many of our horses and cattle in Wallowa, and we lost several hundred in crossing the river. All my people succeeded in getting across in safety. Many of the Nez Percés came together in Rocky Canon to hold a grand council. I went with all my people. This council lasted ten days. There was a great deal of war talk and a great deal of excitement. There was one young brave present whose father had been killed by a white man five years before. This man's blood was bad against white men and he left the council calling for revenge.

Again I counseled peace, and I thought the danger was past. We had not complied with General Howard's order because we could not, but we intended to do so as soon as possible. I was leaving the council to kill beef for my family when news came that the young man whose father had been killed had gone out with several hot-blooded young braves and killed four white men. He rode up to the council and shouted: "Why do you sit here like women? The war has begun already." I was deeply grieved. All the lodges were moved except my brother's and my own. I saw clearly that the war was upon us when I learned that my young men had been secretly buying ammunition. I heard then that Too-hul-hul-sote, who had been imprisoned by General Howard, had succeeded in organizing a war party. I knew that their acts would involve all my people. I saw that the war could not then be prevented. The time had passed. I counseled peace from the beginning. I knew that we were too weak to fight the United States. We had many grievances, but I knew that war would bring more. We had good white friends, who advised us against taking the war-path. My friend and brother, Mr. Chapman, who has been with us since the surrender, told us just how the war would end. Mr. Chapman took sides against us and helped General Howard. I do not blame him for doing so. He tried hard to prevent bloodshed. We hoped the white settlers would not join the soldiers. Before the war commenced we had discussed this matter all over, and many of my people were in favor of warning them that if they took no part against us they should not be molested in the event of war being begun by General Howard. This plan was voted down in the war-council.

There were bad men among my people who had quarreled with white men, and they talked of their wrongs until they roused all the bad hearts in the council. Still I could not believe that they would begin the war. I know that my young men did a great wrong, but I ask, Who was first to blame? They had been insulted a thousand times; their fathers and brothers had been killed; their mothers and wives had been disgraced; they had been driven to madness by the whiskey sold to them by the white men; they had been told by General Howard that all their horses and cattle which they had been unable to drive out of Wallowa were to fall into the hands of white men; and, added to all this, they were homeless and desperate.

I would have given my own life if I could have undone the killing of white men by my people. I blame my young men and I blame the white men. I blame General Howard for not giving my people time to get their stock away from Wallowa. I do not acknowledge that he had the right to order me to leave Wallowa at any time. I deny that either my father or myself ever sold that land. It is still our land. It may never again be our home, but my father sleeps there, and I love it as I love my mother. I left there, hoping to avoid bloodshed.

If General Howard had given me plenty of time to gather up my stock, and treated Too-hul-hul-sote as a man should be treated, there would have been no war. My friends among white men have blamed me for the war. I am not to blame. When my young men began the killing, my heart was hurt. Although I did not justify them, I remembered all the insults I had endured, and my blood was on fire. Still I would have taken my people to the buffalo country without fighting, if possible.

I could see no other way to avoid a war. We moved over to White Bird Creek, sixteen miles away, and there encamped, intending to collect our stock before leaving; but the soldiers attacked us and the first battle was fought. We numbered in that battle sixty men, and the soldiers a hundred. The fight lasted but a few minutes, when the soldiers retreated before us for twelve miles. They lost thirty-three killed, and had seven wounded. When an Indian fights, he only shoots to kill; but soldiers shoot at random. None of the soldiers were scalped. We do not believe in scalping, nor in killing wounded men. Soldiers do not kill many Indians unless they are wounded and left upon the battlefield. Then they kill Indians.

Seven days after the first battle General Howard arrived in the Nez Percés country, bringing seven hundred more soldiers. It was now war in earnest. We crossed over Salmon River, hoping General Howard would follow. We were not disappointed. He did follow us, and we got between him and his supplies, and cut him off for three days. He sent out two companies to open the way. We attacked them, killing one officer, two guides, and ten men.

We withdrew, hoping the soldiers would follow, but they had got fighting enough for that day. They intrenched themselves, and next day we attacked them again. The battle lasted all day, and was renewed next morning. We killed four and wounded seven or eight.

About this time General Howard found out that we were in his rear. Five days later he attacked us with three hundred and fifty soldiers and settlers. We had two hundred and fifty warriors. The fight lasted twenty-seven hours. We lost four killed and several wounded. General Howard's loss was twenty-nine men killed and sixty wounded.

The following day the soldiers charged upon us, and we retreated with our families and stock a few miles, leaving eighty lodges to fall into General Howard's hands.

Finding that we were outnumbered, we retreated to Bitter Root Valley. Here another body of soldiers came upon us and demanded our surrender. We refused. They said, "You cannot get by us." We answered, "We are going by you without fighting if you will let us, but we are going by you anyhow." We then made a treaty with these soldiers. We agreed not to molest any one and they agreed that we might pass through the Bitter Root country in peace. We bought provisions and traded stock with white men there.

We understood that there was to be no war. We intended to go peaceably to the buffalo country, and leave the question of returning to our country to be settled afterward.

With this understanding we traveled on for four days, and, thinking that the trouble was all over, we stopped and prepared tent-poles to take with us. We started again, and at the end of two days we saw three white men passing our camp. Thinking that peace had been made, we did not molest them. We could have killed, or taken them prisoners, but we did not suspect them of being spies, which they were.

That night the soldiers surrounded our camp. About daybreak one of my men went out to look after his horses. The soldiers saw him and shot him down like a coyote. I have since learned that these soldiers were not those we had left behind. They had come upon us from another direction. The new white warchief's name was Gibbon. He charged upon us while some of my people were still asleep. We had a hard fight. Some of my men crept around and attacked the soldiers from the rear. In this battle we lost nearly all our lodges, but we finally drove General Gibbon back.

Finding that he was not able to capture us, he sent to his camp a few miles away for his big guns (cannons), but my men had captured them and all the ammunition. We damaged the big guns all we could, and carried away the powder and lead. In the fight with General Gibbon we lost fifty women and children and thirty fighting men. We remained long enough to bury our dead. The Nez Percés never make war on women and children; we could have killed a great many women and children while the war lasted, but we would feel ashamed to do so cowardly an act.

We never scalp our enemies, but when General Howard came up and joined General Gibbon, their Indian scouts dug up our dead and scalped them. I have been told that General Howard did not order this great shame to be done.

We retreated as rapidly as we could toward the buffalo country. After six days General Howard came close to us, and we went out and attacked him, and captured nearly all his horses and mules (about two hundred and fifty head). We then marched on to the Yellowstone Basin.

On the way we captured one white man and two white women. We released them at the end of three days. They were treated kindly. The women were not insulted. Can the white soldiers tell me of one time when Indian women were taken prisoners, and held three days and then released without being insulted? Were the Nez Percés women who fell into the hands of General Howard's soldiers treated with as much respect? I deny that a Nez Percé was ever guilty of such a crime.

A few days later we captured two more white men. One of them stole a horse and escaped. We gave the other a poor horse and told him that he was free.

Nine days' march brought us to the mouth of Clarke's Fork of the Yellowstone. We did not know what had become of General Howard, but we supposed that he had sent for more horses and mules. He did not come up, but another new war-chief (General Sturgis) attacked us. We held him in check while we moved all our women and children and stock out of danger, leaving a few men to cover our retreat.

Several days passed, and we heard nothing of Generals Howard, or Gibbon, or Sturgis. We had repulsed each in turn, and began to feel secure, when another army, under General Miles, struck us. This was the fourth army, each of which outnumbered our fighting force, that we had encountered within sixty days.

We had no knowledge of General Miles' army until a short time before he made a charge upon us, cutting our camp in two, and capturing nearly all of our horses. About seventy men, myself among them, were cut off. My little daughter, twelve years of age, was with me. I gave her a rope, and told her to catch a horse and join the others who were cut off from the camp. I have not seen her since, but I have learned that she is alive and well.

I thought of my wife and children, who were now surrounded by soldiers, and I resolved to go to them or die. With a prayer in my mouth to the Great Spirit Chief who rules above, I dashed unarmed through the line of soldiers. It seemed to me that there were guns on every side, before and behind me. My clothes were cut to pieces and my horse was wounded, but I was not hurt. As I reached the door of my lodge, my wife handed me my rifle, saying: "Here's your gun. Fight!"

The soldiers kept up a continuous fire. Six of my men were killed in one spot near me. Ten or twelve soldiers charged into our camp and got possession of two lodges, killing three Nez Percés and losing three of their men, who fell inside our lines. I called my men to drive them back. We fought at close range, not more than twenty steps apart, and drove the soldiers back upon their main line, leaving their dead in our hands. We secured their arms and ammunition. We lost, the first day and night, eighteen men and three women. General Miles lost twenty-six killed and forty wounded. The following day General Miles sent a messenger into my camp under protection of a white flag. I sent my friend Yellow Bull to meet him.

Yellow Bull understood the messenger to say that General Miles wished me to consider the situation; that he did not want to kill my people unnecessarily. Yellow Bull understood this to be a demand for me to surrender and save blood. Upon reporting this message to me, Yellow Bull said he wondered whether General Miles was in earnest. I sent him back with my answer, that I had not made up my mind, but would think about it and send word soon. A little later he sent some Cheyenne scouts with another message. I went out to meet them. They said they believed that General Miles was sincere and really wanted peace. I walked on to General Miles' tent. He met me and we shook hands. He said, "Come, let us sit down by the fire and talk this matter over." I remained with him all night;

next morning, Yellow Bull came over to see if I was alive, and why I did not return.

General Miles would not let me leave the tent to see my friend alone.

Yellow Bull said to me: "They have got you in their power, and I am afraid they will never let you go again. I have an officer in our camp, and I will hold him until they let you go free."

I said: "I do not know what they mean to do with me, but if they kill me you must not kill the officer. It will do no good to avenge my death by killing him."

Yellow Bull returned to my camp. I did not make any agreement that day with General Miles. The battle was renewed while I was with him. I was very anxious about my people. I knew that we were near Sitting Bull's camp in King George's land, and I thought maybe the Nez Percés who had escaped would return with assistance. No great damage was done to either party during the night.

On the following morning I returned to my camp by agreement, meeting the officer who had been held a prisoner in my camp at the flag of truce. My people were divided about surrendering. We could have escaped from Bear Paw Mountain if we had left our wounded, old women, and children behind. We were unwilling to do this. We had never heard of a wounded Indian recovering while in the hands of white men.

On the evening of the fourth day, General Howard came in with a small escort, together with my friend Chapman. We could talk now understandingly. General Miles said to me in plain words, "If you will come out and give up your arms, I will spare your lives and send you back to the reservation." I do not know what passed between General Miles and General Howard.

I could not bear to see my wounded men and women suffer any longer; we had lost enough already. General Miles had promised that we might return to our country with what stock we had left. I thought we could start again. I believed General Miles, or I never would have surrendered. I have heard that he has been censured for making the promise to return us to

Lapwai. He could not have made any other terms with me at that time. I would have held him in check until my friends came to my assistance, and then neither of the generals nor their soldiers would have ever left Bear Paw Mountain alive.

On the fifth day I went to General Miles and gave up my gun, and said, "From where the sun now stands I will fight no more." My people needed rest—we wanted peace.

I was told we could go with General Miles to Tongue River and stay there until spring, when we would be sent back to our country. Finally it was decided that we were to be taken to Tongue River. We had nothing to say about it. After our arrival at Tongue River, General Miles received orders to take us to Bismarck. The reason given was that subsistence would be cheaper there.

General Miles was opposed to this order. He said: "You must not blame me. I have endeavored to keep my word, but the chief who is over me has given the order, and I must obey it or resign. That would do you no good. Some other officer would carry out the order."

I believe General Miles would have kept his word if he could have done so. I do not blame him for what we have suffered since the surrender. I do not know who is to blame. We gave up all our horses—over eleven hundred—and all our saddles— over one hundred—and we have not heard from them since. Somebody has got our horses.

General Miles turned my people over to another soldier, and we were taken to Bismarck. Captain Johnson, who now had charge of us, received an order to take us to Fort Leavenworth. At Leavenworth we were placed in on a low river bottom, with no water except river water to drink and cook with. We had always lived in a healthy country, where the mountains were high and the water was cold and clear. Many of our people sickened and died, and we buried them in this strange land.* I cannot tell how much my heart suffered for my people while at Leavenworth. The Great Spirit Chief who rules above seemed to be looking some other way, and did not see what was being done to my people.

---

*I can corroborate this. I saw them there often.—C. T. B.

During the hot days (July, 1878) we received notice that we were to be moved farther away from our own country. We were not asked if we were willing to go. We were ordered to get into the railroad cars. Three of my people died on the way to Baxter Springs. It was worse to die there than to die fighting in the mountains.

We were moved from Baxter Springs (Kansas) to the Indian Territory and set down without our lodges. We had but little medicine and we were nearly all sick. Seventy of my people have died since we moved there.

We have had a great many visitors who have talked many ways. Some of the chiefs (General Fish and Colonel Stickney) from Washington came to see us, and selected land for us to live upon. We have not moved to that land, for it is not a good place to live.

The Commissioner Chief (E. A. Hayt) came to see us. I told him, as I told every one, that I expected General Miles' word would be carried out. He said it "could not be done; that white men now lived in my country and all the land was taken up; that, if I returned to Wallowa, I could not live in peace; that law-papers were out against my young men who began the war, and that the Government could not protect my people." This talk fell like a heavy stone upon my heart. I saw that I could not gain anything by talking to him. Other law chiefs (Congressional Committee) came to see us and said they would help me to get a healthy country. I did not know whom to believe. The white people have too many chiefs. They do not understand each other. They do not talk alike.

The Commissioner Chief (Mr. Hayt) invited me to go with him and hunt for a better home than we have now. I like the land we found (west of the Osage Reservation) better than any place I have seen in that country; but it is not a healthy land. There are no mountains and rivers. The water is warm. It is not a good country for stock. I do not believe my people can live there. I am afraid they will all die. The Indians who occupy that country are dying off. I promised Chief Hayt to go there, and do the best I could until the Government got ready to make good General Miles' word. I was not satisfied, but I could not help myself.

Then the Inspector Chief (General McNiel) came to my camp and we had a long talk. He said I ought to have a home in the mountain country north, and that he would write a letter to the Great Chief in Washington. Again the hope of seeing the mountains of Idaho and Oregon grew up in my heart.

At last I was granted permission to come to Washington and bring my friend Yellow Bull and our interpreter with me. I am glad we came. I have shaken hands with a great many friends, but there are some things I want to know which no one seems able to explain. I cannot understand how the Government sends a man out to fight us, as it did General Miles, and then breaks his word. Such a Government has something wrong about it. I cannot understand why so many chiefs are allowed to talk so many different ways, and promise so many different things. I have seen the Great Father Chief (the President); the next Great Chief (Secretary of the Interior); the Commissioner Chief (Hayt); the Law Chief (General Butler), and many other law chiefs (Congressmen), and they all say they are my friends, and that I shall have justice, but while their mouths all talk right I do not understand why nothing is done for my people. I have heard talk and talk, but nothing is done. Good words do not last long until they amount to something. Words do not pay for my dead people. They do not pay for my country, now overrun by white men. They do not protect my father's grave. They do not pay for my horses and cattle. Good words will not give me back my children. Good words will not make good the promise of your War Chief, General Miles. Good words will not give my people good health and stop them from dying. Good words will not get my people a home where they can live in peace and take care of themselves. I am tired of talk that comes to nothing. It makes my heart sick when I remember all the good words and all the broken promises. There has been too much talking by men who had no right to talk. Too many misrepresentations have been made, too many misunderstandings have come up between the white men about the Indians. If the white man wants to live in peace with the Indian he can live in peace. There need

29

be no trouble. Treat all men alike. Give them all the same law. Give them all an even chance to live and grow. All men were made by the same Great Spirit Chief. They are all brothers. The earth is the mother of all people, and all people should have equal rights upon it. You might as well expect the rivers to run backward as that any man who was born a free man should be contented penned up and denied liberty to go where he pleases. If you tie a horse to a stake, do you expect he will grow fat? If you pen an Indian up on a small spot of earth, and compel him to stay there, he will not be contented nor will he grow and prosper. I have asked some of the great white chiefs where they get their authority to say to the Indian that he shall stay in one place, while he sees white men going where they please. They cannot tell me.

I only ask of the Government to be treated as all other men are treated. If I cannot go to my own home, let me have a home in some country where my people will not die so fast. I would like to go to Bitter Root Valley. There my people would be healthy; where they are now they are dying. Three have died since I left my camp to come to Washington.

When I think of our condition my heart is heavy. I see men of my race treated as outlaws and driven from country to country, or shot down like animals.

I know that my race must change. We cannot hold our own with the white men as we are. We only ask an even chance to live as other men live. We ask to be recognized as men. We ask that the same law shall work alike on all men. If the Indian breaks the law, punish him by the law. If the white man breaks the law, punish him also.

Let me be a free man—free to travel, free to stop, free to work, free to trade, where I choose, free to choose my own teachers, free to follow the religion of my fathers, free to think and talk and act for myself—and I will obey every law, or submit to the penalty.

Whenever the white man treats the Indian as they treat each other, then we shall have no more wars. We shall be all alike— brothers of one father and one mother, with one sky above us and one country around us, and one government for all. Then the Great Spirit Chief who rules above will smile upon this land, and send rain to wash out the bloody spots made by brothers' hands upon the face of the earth. For this time the Indian race are waiting and praying. I hope that no more groans of wounded men and women will ever go to the ear of the Great Spirit Chief above, and that all people may be one people.

In-mut-too-yah-lat-lat has spoken for his people.

Young Joseph.

Article by Soy (Keith) Redthunder

In the time since 1877, many changes have occurred to the Nez Perce people. For the historians, the Nez Perce people represented a fragmented and divided people. For the Nez Perce people themselves, they are a people who have tolerated many unkept promises and much degradation. Our people were separated and never able to enjoy the pride, joy, and feeling of belonging as a total people. Although many attempts have been made to restrict it, kinship continues to thrive. We, as a people, survive even though we have been taught different ways.

When the Nez Perce first met the white man, their intentions were never questioned or suspected. Lewis and Clark were very grateful to have that kind of trust. Many of the first greetings to the white man were of respect. Many events led to the distrust from both sides, and finally to the "War" which nobody wanted. The teachings of the Great Spirit to the Indians were: treat each other good; never lie to each other; always respect what the creator has left for us. These and other ways to live are still relevant in today's world. However, we find living in this world very difficult.

Many historians consider Chief Joseph a military genius. It may by a point in fact that Chief Joseph be remembered more for being a chief humanitarian. For it was he who became more responsible for the survival of his band of people than as a military genius. For this, we, as a people, should be very grateful. Chalo.

Soy or Keith Redthunder's father is Joe Redthunder, great grandson of Chief Joseph.

31

CHIEF LOOKING GLASS
Photo credit, Washington State University, Pullman, WA.
Historical Photograph Collections, Neg. #78-152.

NOTES

There were two Chief Josephs, father and son. Chief Joseph the elder was born about 1790 and died in 1870. He was the son of a Nez Perce chief and became chief by right of succession, this about 1832, or about four years before the first Protestant missionaries, Marcus Whitman and Henry Harmon Spaulding, came to the inland Pacific Northwest. He was friendly toward whites but insisted that they not settle in his homeland, the Wallowa valley. He signed the treaty of 1855 with Isaac Stevens which gave his people the Wallowa valley forever. Forever in this case lasted twenty-two years. His body lies in the Indian burying ground overlooking the Wallowa lake.

Chief Joseph the younger was born about 1840 and died September 21, 1904, on the Colville Indian reservation. His Indian name was *In-mut-too-yah-lat-lat,* which is translated as "Thunder traveling over the mountains", but he was commonly known as Chief Joseph. He refused with his father to recognize the treaty of 1863 and declined to move his people to the Nez Perce reservation at Lapwai, Idaho, basing this refusal on the earlier treaty which gave his people their land in the Wallowas.

Although personally opposed to violence he fought for the right of his Nez Perce to hold their Wallowa land. He was a political rather than a military leader but when war broke out he cast his lot with his own people and they made an arduous 1300 mile retreat across the mountains of central Idaho and western Montana attempting to reach Canada. This long retreat was made encumbered by women, children, livestock and personal possessions. It was masterfully managed and was stopped by Nelson A. Miles just short of the Canadian border. Actually some Nez Perce managed to reach Canada. Joseph was a gifted orator and an acknowledged leader of his people, a man respected by both Indians and whites. His booklet is not completely accurate but here is Indian history in Chief Joseph's own words and as he sincerely believed. This material is now fairly difficult to obtain.

Chief Joseph's Own Story first appeared in the North American Review for April, 1879.

Glen Adams, printer
Fairfield, Washington
August 27, 1973.

CHIEF OLLOCOT
Photo credit, Washington State University, Pullman, WA.
Historical Photograph Collections, Neg. #82-019.

Oliver Otis Howard

November 8, 1830 — October 26, 1909

Nelson Appleton Miles

August 8, 1839 — May 15, 1925

Index

A

Adams, Glen..................34,35
Ahlokat, (Nez Perce)..............36
American Fights and Fighters, Brady.........4n.

B

Baxter Springs, Kansas................6,28
Bear Paw Mountains...............3,26.27
Big Hole........................3
Bismarck, N.D. 27
Bitter Root Valley.................23,30
Black Buffalo, Chief................5n.
Brady, Cyrus Townsend.......4n.,7,7n.,11n,35
Butler, General 29

C

Camas Meadows 6
Canada 3,6,34
Chapman, Arthur I................21,26
Cheyenne Indians 25
Chinook, Montana 3
Chute-pa-lu, (Nez Perces).............11
Clarke's Fork 24
Colville Reservation.........6-7,33,frontis
Cummin's Indian Congress............7

D

Declaration of Independence............9
Dunn, J.P. ....7n.

E

Edwards, Governor.................5n.

F

Fish, General 28
Fort Lapwai......................17
Fort Leavenworth.................6,27
Fort Walla Walla..................19
Frenchmen.......................12

G

Gibbon, General John..............3,23-24
Great Northern R.R................3,35
Great Spirit, Chief.........9,11,17,25,30,31
Great White Chief (President)........15,27,29
Gibbon, General John..............3,23-34
Great Northern R.R................3,35
Great Spirit, Chief.........9,11,17,25,30,31
Great White Chief (President)........15,27,29

H

Hare, Rt. Rev. W.H. 7,10
Hayt, E.A. 28,29
Henry Lake 6
Howard General Oliver O. 3,4,6,8,11n., 17-18,19,20,21,22,23,24,26,37

I

Idaho 29,34
Indian Territory...................28
In-mut-too-yah-lat-lat (cf. Chief Joseph).......11, 31,33

J

Joseph, Chief (Old) 4-5,9,11,12,13,14,15,33
Joseph, Young Chief ......frontis, 1,2,3-7,7-10,11, 16,31,33-34
Johnson, Capt....................27

K

King George's land (Canada)..............26

L

Lapwai Reservation.........14,15,16,19,20,27,33
Lawyer, Chief 14
Lewis and Clark Expedition.............12
Lolo Trail 3
Looking Glass, Chief 4,19,32

M

McNiel, General 29
MacRae, Donald 3
Madison Square Gardens 7
Maha Indians . . . . .5n.
Massacres of the Mountains, Dunn . . . . .7n.
Miles, Col. Nelson A. (Gen.) 3,6,7,9,10,
    24-27,28,29,34,38
Milk River 3
Miller, Col. . . . . .5n.
Mississippi River . . . . .5n.
Missouri River . . . . .3,5n.
Montana 6,34

N

New York Sun 4
Nez Perce Indians 3,5,6,8,11,12,13,14,16,20,
    24,25,26,33,34
Nez Perce War 4,5,6,7
Non-Treaty Indians 5,13,14
North American Review, The 7n.,9,34,35

O

Ollicut (Joseph's brother) 4
Oregon 5,11,29
Osage Reservation 28

P

Portage des Sioux 5

R

Rocky Canyon 20
Rocky Mountains 6

S

Salmon River 8,22
Sherman, General W.T. 6
Sitting Bull, Chief 3,26
Snake Creek 3
Snake River 19
South Dakota, Bishop of 7
Spalding, Rev. H.H. 5,11,12,13

Standing Elk, Chief . . . . .5n.
Stevens, Gov. I.I. 13,33
Stickney, Col. 28
Sturgis, Col. Samuel (Gen.) 24

T

Teton Indians . . . . .5n.
Thunder-traveling-over-the-mountains . . . .
    (Chief Joseph's Indian name trans.) 11,33
Tongue River 27
Too-hul-hul-sote (Nez Perce) 4,18-19,20,21,
    22
Treaty Indians .13,14,16
Treaty of 1855 . . . . .11n.,13,18
Treaty of 1863 14,33

U

Umatilla Agency 17
United States Government 10,13,14,16,17,
    21,28,29,30
United States troops 4,8,17

V

Valley of the Winding Waters (Wallowa) 6,9,
    15,20,33

W

Wal-lam-wat-kin Band 11
Walla Walla, W.T. 17
Wallowa (cf. Valley of Winding Water) 14,16,
    17,19,20,21,28,33,34
Wallowa Lake 33
Washington, D.C. 7,11,29,30
Washington (State) 6
Washington State University 1,32
Western Magazine 2
White Bird, Chief 19
White Bird Creek 22
Whitemen 11-16,19,20,21,23,24,26,28,29,30,

Y

Yellow Bull (Nez Perce) 25-26,29
Yellowstone Basin 24
Yellowstone River 24

COLOPHON

CHIEF JOSEPH'S OWN STORY was printed in the *NORTH AMERICAN REVIEW* for April, 1879, and then reprinted in the Cyrus Townsend Brady, *FIGHTS AND FIGHTERS*, July 1907. The booklet was printed again by Glen Adams in September, 1973, and then again several times since. Taken from the original *Great Northern Railroad* edition, and has sold out in seven consecutive printings. This is now the eighth Ye Galleon printing of the Chief Joseph booklet to come from the workshop of Ye Galleon Press, which is located in the quiet country village of Fairfield, southern Spokane County in Washington state. Additional typesetting was done by Teresa Ruggles. Photography and film stripping was done by Dustin Newlun. Printing plates were made by Garry Adams. Printing was done by Trevor Del Medico using a Heidelberg press, model KORS. Folding and assembly was done by the Ye Galleon staff. This was a fun project. We had no special difficulties with the work.